ublished by

ONGSTREET PRESS, INC.

ubsidiary of Cox Newspapers, Inc.

0 Newmarket Parkway

te 118

ietta, GA 30067

the United States of America

g 1992

ongress Catalog Card Number: 92-71794

2-049-4

rinted by R. R. Donnelley & Sons, Harrisonburg,
xt was set in Bookman.

Lee Holbrook

Ludlow Porch by Floyd Jillson

ag courtesy of the Georgia Deparment of

m

ura McDonald

Beating a D[...]
Horse is Mo[...]
Than You[...]

A Parti[...]
of th[...]

Lu[...]

P[...]
LC[...]
A s[...]
214[...]
Sui[...]
Mar[...]

Copy[...]

Printed in[...]

1st printing[...]

Library of C[...]

ISBN 1-5635[...]

This book was p[...]
Virginia. The t[...]

Jacket design b[...]
Jacket photo of[...]
Jacket photo of f[...]
Trade and Touris[...]
Book design by La[...]

This book is dedicated to
General Robert E. Lee
1807 - 1870

TABLE of CONTENTS

INTRODUCTION

Some who read the following pages will encounter sentiments that might not be considered politically correct. Let me quickly assure those readers that what they will find here is not anti-anything. Others will want to accuse me of beating a dead horse; they'll wonder why I don't just hush up about my native Southland. But for those who love the South like I do, beating this old dead horse is more fun than yankee-watching out at the Stuckey's on the highway. So here it is—my tribute to a place and its people that hold a special place in my heart.

What the South is about, as I see it, is live oak trees, Florida's beautiful Indian River, and Atlanta Cracker baseball.

It's about cornbread, fried chicken, Coca-Cola, and dawn in Laurel, Mississippi.

It's about *our* song, "Dixie," which gives me cold chills whenever I hear it.

It's about Minnie Pearl, Daytona Beach, and dove hunting.

It's about old men who chew tobacco and children who say, "Yes ma'am" and "No ma'am."

It's about Knoxville and meatskins and the smell of honeysuckle.

It's about Martin Luther King, Thomas Jefferson, and Jimmy Carter.

It's about Peachtree Street in the rain,

Spanish moss, and Jack Daniels.

It's about the French Quarter, the Gator Bowl, and Louis Armstrong.

It's about the people in Madison, Georgia; Decatur, Alabama; and Spartanburg, South Carolina.

It's about 500 acres of snow-white cotton and the Grand Ole Opry.

I thank the Almighty that I was one of those chosen to "live and die in Dixie."

SOUTHERN
★ FACES ★

★ THE SOUTHERN BELLE ★

In the South, we have always been proud of our women. A quick survey by even a nearsighted person will prove what I have always known. Southern women are the most beautiful in the world. Stand on any street corner in the Deep South and you will find that about seventy percent of the Southern Belles you see are drop-dead beautiful, and the other thirty percent could win the Miss Ohio beauty contest by just showing up.

Over the decades, the beauty of Southern women has inspired songs, poems, and novels. In the Old South, even a hint of an insult toward a young lady could result in a duel. Just the sound of their names conjures up images of beauty, charm, and grace: Patsy Jean, Amber, Betty Jo, and, of course, Scarlett.

However, it takes more than beauty, charm, grace, and a name to make one a true Southern

Belle. There is a strict—and I mean strict—code of conduct that every true Southern Belle adheres to. The code is not written down anywhere. It can only be learned at the knee of a Southern Belle mama. Once learned, however, the code is never violated. The penalty for violation is to be thought forward, brazen, or brash, or, in the case of the most flagrant violation, to be deemed "common white trash."

Southern Belles have a long list of things that they never do. This list is not written down anywhere either, but is as much a part of their lives as "the vapors." Let's take a look at some of the things true Belles would never do.

- Southern Belles never smoke on the street. There are no rules against smoking, but very strict rules about where they may smoke. It is perfectly all right to smoke in a restaurant as long as they are sitting down. They must never be seen standing or walking with a cigarette in their hand. When in public, they must never light their own cigarette. For a true Southern Belle, there will always be someone near at hand to take care of that small task.

- A Southern Belle never goes into a bar or lounge without an escort. And

once there, she never tries to impress
her date by showing him how she can
tie a knot in a cherry stem with her
tongue.

- A true Southern Belle would never, and
I mean never, scold or speak harshly
to a waiter or waitress. There are no
exceptions. If a waitress should spill
a pitcher of Salty Dogs in her lap, the
true Belle will smile sweetly and say,
"Let me hep you clean that up, sugar."
Never in her life will a Southern Belle
be rude to someone acting in a service
capacity. In a bar or restaurant, a
true Southern Belle would no more
speak loudly than she would order a
vodka shooter. If word ever got out that
she was drinking tequila, sucking a
piece of lime, and licking salt off the
back of her hand, she would be thrown
out of the Junior League before you
could say "Montgomery, Alabama."
And she would never drink anything
out of a can—no place, no way, no how.

- In a restaurant, the Southern Belle will
always order the middle-priced item on
the menu. If she orders the cheapest
thing, she might leave the impres-

sion that she thinks her date can't afford to be there. If she orders the most expensive thing, he might think she is too extravagant. Once her dinner has arrived, she knows not to eat everything on her plate. Just like her mama told her, she will always leave something on the plate for Mr. Manners.

- A Southern Belle would never call a man outside of her family on the phone. There are only three exceptions to this rule: a fireman, a policeman, or her doctor— and even in these cases she would prefer that a woman answer. She would rather die a slow, painful death than carry a white purse or wear white shoes before Easter or after Labor Day. She would never wear gloves without a hat.

- When she gets on an airplane, she is dressed with the same formality that she would be dressed for her funeral.

- When she gets married, she wears a white wedding dress. This rule holds even if she has been to bed with every member of the Atlanta Falcons and two guys she met at a Burger King drive-thru window.

- She would never hurt anyone's feelings intentionally, but when angered, she can deliver a tongue-lashing that would bring the Devil himself to his knees.

- A Southern Belle never sweats. It simply is not done. Nor does she whistle. The last time she tried was when she was six years old. Her mother told her, "A whistling girl and a crowing hen never come to no good end." She never whistled again.

- She would never talk about another man with the man she is with. She would never eat a raw weenie in public. She would never spit, request a Jerry Lee Lewis record be played at her wedding reception, or put sugar in her cornbread.

- She would never date a man named Three-Fingered Jerome, sit spraddle-legged, or take lasagna to a church covered-dish supper.

She is a delight, a wonder, and a mystery, but most importantly, she's ours.

★ WHITE TRASH ★

The world would be a pretty dull place without white trash. They are about the only large group left that you can make fun of and not be considered politically incorrect. You can openly say anything you want to about white trash and nobody gets upset. It's not that they are tolerant; it's just that white trash don't know they are white trash.

In my more than twenty years on the air, I have told many "white trash" stories. I have referred to them many, many times in less than flattering terms. Not one time has anybody ever called my boss and said, "I'm white trash and Ludlow is on the radio making fun of me."

In discussing this sub-species, the first myth we must dispose of is that being white trash is somehow related to your station in life or your income. In the South, we know that wealth or position in the community has nothing to do with being white trash.

I once knew the secretary/treasurer of a huge, successful bakery. He made the big bucks, drove a Cadillac and was the choir director at his church. It turned out that he was also three things that nobody suspected. He was an embezzler, he was a womanizer (fooling around with the church organist), and he was white trash. The congressmen who were caught in Abscam were all white trash.

For the reader's edification, here are twenty-five defining characteristics of white trash:

- White trash men all refer to their wives as "my old lady," and white trash wives call their husbands "my old man."

- White trash must have at least one relative named for an animal. Some of the more common examples are Possum, Pig, Buck, Snake, Weasel, Rooster, Cooter, Goat, Junebug, Red Dog, Pony, Bird, Squirrel, Frog, Rabbit, Gator, Ox, Spider, Wormy, Mule, and Bug. I once knew of a white trash family who nicknamed their oldest daughter "Dog Breath."

- While there are exceptions, generally speaking, white trash will not marry blood relatives closer than nephews.

- White trash do not change their babies' diapers on any day with a "U" in it.

- Survey after survey has shown that white trash make up 87.6 percent of the U.S. toothpick market. This statistic seems accurate when you realize that most adult male white trash (and many female) keep a toothpick hanging out of their mouth during all their waking hours.

- The first three words that white trash children learn to say are "mama," "daddy," and "shit," not necessarily in that order.

- White trash think that any joke about a bathroom or a body function is funny.

- At least one member of a white trash family must have the surname "Junior."

- White trash cars will not run without some type of fuzzy object hanging from their rearview mirror (if they have a rearview mirror).

- White trash do not consider the dog to be man's best friend. They regard the jumper cable as man's best friend.

- Seventy-eight percent of white trash have been fingerprinted by their seventeenth birthday.

- The code of the white trash requires that anytime they attend a sporting event, they must be dog drunk prior to the end of the national anthem.

- While all white trash men are not wife beaters, all wife beaters are white trash.

- Not all white trash are white.

- White trash are generally kind to their dogs. They usually provide a large oil spill for them to lie in.

- The favorite mode of transportation for white trash is any vehicle with not more than three fenders.

- White trash prefer to use their front porches to store their worn-out kitchen appliances.

- White trash children must start using some type of tobacco by age twelve.

- White trash consider chickens to be house pets.

- White trash only park in handicapped parking spaces.

- White trash are the exclusive market for white sidewall tire planters.

- White trash consider abandoned cars to be an important part of their landscape architecture.

- White trash can not understand why a professional wrestler has never been appointed to the supreme court.

- White trash always seem to have cold heads. You can prove that by noticing that they all eat with their hats on.

- White trash consider any car with lawn furniture in the back to be a limo.

I don't want to leave the impression that some have not risen to great heights. They have become generals, presidents of large corporations, and dictators of countries. At least two of them have actually appeared in the famous Robert L. Ripley's newspaper feature "Believe It or Not"—one of them for being an only child, and another for having liability insurance on his car.

YOU'RE IN A HEAP OF
★ TROUBLE, BOY ★

Southern policemen are a wonderful part of every Southerner's life. They are a breed unto themselves. They are not only keepers of the peace; they are our friends and neighbors, and they are the butt of many of our jokes.

Some of the most interesting characters I have ever known have worn a badge. There was a policeman in my youth who was a legend to me and my peers. I will simply call him Buster.

He was small for a Southern cop, about 5'6" tall, and weighed about 140 pounds. What he lacked in size, however, he made up in pure rattlesnake meanness. It was said that Buster would fight a circle saw and spot it the first two licks. His claim to fame, however, was not his size or his meanness; it was his prowess with a blackjack.

The story was that one dark night, a group of the local good old boys were having a crap game in the living room of one of their homes. They were so into the rolling of the bones that they didn't even notice Buster walk quietly into the room. In a quiet voice, Buster said, "Y'all lay down on the floor. I'm fixin' to take this whole lash-up to jail for runnin' a crap game." Everybody complied, except for one old boy who jumped through an open window. Buster was right behind him. The crap shooter was more fleet of foot than little Buster, though, and it soon became apparent to our hero that he was losing ground.

When about half a city block separated them, Buster pulled out his blackjack and threw it like a tomahawk. Witnesses said later that it hit the man in the back of the head and he fell like he had been pole-axed.

Later, knowing of Buster's violent leanings, someone jokingly asked him why he had not shot the suspect. Buster said, "Aw, he's a good old boy . . . besides, I know his daddy."

A city policeman in a small west Georgia town was standing in the middle of the street directing traffic. Right behind him was a larger-than-life-sized statue of a Southern general. A carload of northern tourists stopped for the red light, and, pointing to the statue, the driver asked the officer, "Whose statue is that?"

Without missing a beat, the policeman said, "It's ours."

In a small Tennessee town, the local smokey stopped a car carrying four black men. He waddled up to the car and said, "Where are you fellas from?"

"Chicago," said the driver.

"Oh yeah?" the officer snarled. "If you all are from Chicago, how come you got them Illinois plates on your car?"

In the small town of Abbeville, Louisiana, a burglar alarm sounded in the middle of the night at a warehouse. Two of Abbeville's finest responded. They slid into the parking lot, blue lights flashing and siren screaming. Pistols drawn, one went around the left side of the warehouse and the other went around the right side. They met in back and shot each other.

Buford and Leon, two middle Georgia policemen, stopped a yankee tourist for speeding. The man was very loud and belligerent and insisted the posted speed limit was not 55 mph, but 80. To prove his point, he showed them the sign with that figure on it. Leon said, "That ain't the speed limit; that's the highway number." They gave him a ticket, and as they were walking back to their car, the tourist heard Leon say to Buford, "I'm shore glad we stopped him before he got to 441."

The most typical Southern cop I ever knew or heard about was my boyhood friend "Fats" Funderburk. His real name, of course, was not "Fats," but since he weighed about 240 pounds when we were in the seventh grade, "Fats" was all he had ever been called. I had not seen or heard from him in about twenty years, but through the grapevine, I had heard that he was a captain on a suburban Atlanta police force.

My cousin Doodle was a mechanic and part-time race car driver. He was also the proud owner of a souped-up Corvette. He needed to borrow my larger four-door car to pick up some visitors at the airport, so I went to his house to exchange cars. Doodle is a very hospitable man, and while I was at his house, he held a gun on me and insisted that I have two drinks before I left.

When it was time to go, he went outside with me to show me how to drive his "faster than lightning" Corvette. When I cranked it up, I had never heard such power; even idling, it sounded like it could go 200 hundred miles an hour in "Park." It was by far the most powerful machine I had ever been around. I didn't mind because the two drinks had made me relaxed and confident that I could handle anything.

Driving home, I had on the radio and both windows open. It happened just as I got on the entrance ramp to the expressway. The wind was in my face and Hank Williams on the radio was singing, "If you got the money, Honey, I got the time." Suddenly, without warning, I became sixteen years old again. I started to sing along with old Hank as I mashed the accelerator down, down, down. When the entrance ramp dumped me into the expressway, I was doing about 80 and still singing along with old Hank.

I was just getting to the part about "We'll go honkytonking, and we're going to have a time" when I noticed the blue lights flashing in my rearview mirror. My first thought was "Oh hell! Here I am, whiskey on my breath, speeding, and every blue light in the world going round and round behind me." I pulled over and the blue lights pulled up right behind me. I was looking into my rearview mirror, trying to think up the world's biggest lie, when I saw my boyhood friend "Fats" Funderburk pry himself out of the police car. Even in semi-darkness he was easy to recognize. He had that same unmistakable waddle that he had in the seventh grade. I almost jumped with joy. There was no way that my beloved "Fats" was going to give me a ticket. Why, we had been such good friends that if I had asked, he would have fixed a murder rap for me. I was so happy about my good luck that I decided to have a little fun with my long-lost chum.

I left the motor running because I knew that would irritate him. He was carrying one of those great big old flashlights—the kind with about fifteen batteries. It was the multi-use variety: you could use it to light your way or to hit a suspect upside the head.

He stopped beside my open window but did not bend over to make eye contact. He said, "Let me see your drimen liam." (All Southern policemen call driver's licenses "drimen liam.") I pretended to look for my license while that powerful motor idled louder and louder. I knew it was getting his goat when he started to slap that huge flashlight into his open palm.

"Do you know how fast you was going, Boy?" he asked.

"No, I was down in the engine room at the time," I answered.

"Don't get smart with me, Boy."

"The trouble with you cops," I suggested, "is that you're out here harassing decent citizens when you got lawbreakers double-parked all over town."

"Decent citizens my ass," he said, still trying to control his voice. "You wuz doin' damn near a hundred mile an hour."

When I was sure that he was about to drag

me through the open window, I handed him my license. He saw my name at once and for the first time bent over far enough to look me in the face. He smiled a big toothy grin and said, "You sumbitch . . . where you been?" I got out of the car, and we hugged and shook hands and had a reunion right there on the side of the expressway.

He said, "I just busted a bootlegger, and my patrol car has about two gallons of that old see-through liquor in the trunk. Why don't we have us a little drink?"

The South is full of wonderfully colorful characters—none more colorful than our policemen.

★ FORTUNETELLERS ★

We Southerners are a superstitious crowd. We believe in everything from wart witches to haints. (A haint is a Southern ghost.) We believe that if you step on a crack, your mama is a "goner." We believe that kerosene, when used properly, can cure most of mankind's ills. We believe than a homemade mustard plaster is more effective than open-heart surgery.

We know, for an absolute scientific fact, that cats are bad luck, buckeyes are good luck, and that if you break a mirror your life will not be worth living for seven years.

We are also the home office for fortunetellers nationwide. Any Southerner worth his grits can tell you how to find a fortuneteller who truly has "the gift." If you need to find one, here's how to go about it:

The first thing you look for is a sign; there are two types. One type has the outline of an

Indian head complete with war bonnet. It reads, "Madame Zelda" or "Sister Marie—Indian Advisor and Healer." The other type has the outline of a hand. It reads "Madame Zelda" or "Sister Marie—Palmist and Reader: Knows All, Sees All, and Tells All." Parked close to the sign is a house trailer. I never figured out why, if they knew all and saw all, they had to live in a house trailer. The inside of the trailer is decorated in Early Tacky. It looks like all the furnishings have been won at a county fair.

The fortuneteller always wears very bright clothes and a shawl. Real fortunetellers will own two or three Chihuahua dogs with runny eyes. Everything in the trailer has red ball fringe—the sofa, the chairs, her shawl, and even the Chihuahua.

All fortunetellers are female, and they are all married to gravy-sucking pigs who are too sorry to work. The husband's main function in life seems to be to help his wife hold one of those little, runny-eyed, yappin' dogs. He is always tall and skinny and reminds you of Henry Fonda in *The Grapes of Wrath*.

The cost of the actual reading is only the beginning of your expense. She will always have an extra cost for the product she wants to sell you.

If you are having problems with your love life,

she will sell you a love potion that will make the object of your affection want to cut your lawn, defrost your refrigerator, and kiss you on the mouth.

If you have an enemy, she will sell you a matchbox full of cemetery dirt. All you have to do is sprinkle the dirt on your enemy's property and the wrath of God will descend on that person.

If you find yourself in need of money, she will have charms available that will make you rich beyond your wildest dreams.

In the course of your reading, your friendly neighborhood fortuneteller will tell you how she happened to be blessed with these wonderful powers: she is the seventh daughter of a seventh daughter. She was born with a veil over her face, and she is always one-quarter Cherokee Indian. She was put on this earth to help others, and she will always do whatever she can . . . except give you a free reading.

★ NEW SOUTHERNERS ★

I guess I was about twelve years old before I met someone from the north. A new family moved into my neighborhood with a son about my age named Billy. I liked him at once. It was fun to listen to him talk. I had never known anyone who pronounced his "G"s and who thought a little bitty rock was called a pebble.

In school, he was teased a lot. It hurt his feelings, and because he was my friend, it hurt me too. Now, I'm the first to admit that it's hard not to laugh at someone who thinks gravy is a sauce and a ham biscuit is a little sandwich. Being Southern, however, my mama taught me that it was bad manners to make fun of people, and even worse to laugh out loud at them. In my beloved South, the worst thing that can be said about a person is that he is ill-mannered.

Since the South has become a mecca for people raised in the north, it is important that we not ridicule, but rather attempt to educate them. In an effort to be politically sensitive I have even stopped calling yankees yankees. I have coined the term New Southerners. It seems less harsh and does not conjure up memories of the War between the States. I have put a list together of rules that will help our New Southerners hide the fact that "they ain't from around here."

- We don't care how they did it in Cleveland, Detroit, or Newark. If you really want to tick off a card-carrying, gravy-dipping son of these red clay hills, just tell him how much better things are done in the north.

- Do not talk loud in a restaurant. This advice is particularly good for New Southern women. For some strange reason, they seem to think that everyone in the restaurant should be privy to their conversation. The rule of thumb is that only the people at your table should be able to hear you. If you are unable to speak that softly, then you should just hush.

- Never refer to a soft drink as a soda or a pop. If you want to sound like a native, remember all soft drinks are Coke or Coca-Cola (preferably pronounced Co-Cola).

- All tissue is Kleenex, even if you prefer another brand name. Your conversation with the clerk should go like this: "I'd like a box of Kleenex." The Southern clerk will say, "What kind of Kleenex would you like?" Then and only then do you give him the brand name of your choice. You should also bear in mind that all refrigerators are Frigidaire, all copy machines are Xerox, and all sneakers are tennis shoes.

- Never make any comment, pro or con, about grits. If you like 'em, eat 'em. If you don't, leave 'em alone. To try and tell a Southerner about grits is a perfect example of preachin' to the choir (see "Southern Accents").

- Never try to point out or explain about snow clouds. We don't understand or care about them. If you miss them, go where they are.

- Never eat fried chicken with a knife and fork. If you do, the people around you

will know three things:
   a. You ain't from around here.
   b. You are trying to be uppity.
   c. You don't know nothin' about
      eating fried chicken.

- Never go to a restaurant and order
  blood pudding, lamb, or tongue sandwich. In the first place, they're not
  going to have it. In the second place,
  they're not going to know what you are
  talking about, and in the third place,
  nobody wants a waitress named Flonella
  laughing so hard she spills your water.

- Never blow your car horn. It is much
  better to be killed in a fiery crash than
  to be a bad reflection on your family.
  Horn blowing in the South is considered rude—anytime . . . anyplace . . .
  and under any circumstances.

- Never go out in the snow. Stay home
  and play with your kids. The rule of
  thumb in the South is that any snow
  of one inch or more constitutes a legal
  holiday.

- There are three meals a day: breakfast, dinner, and supper. If you want

lunch, the closest place to get it is Maryland.

- Never refer to the War between the States as the Civil War. In the South, General Sherman taught us that there was nothing civil about that war.

- Never talk about gun control. Put it in the category with politics and religion and leave it out of polite conversation. Remember, New York City has very strict gun control laws.

- Try not to be abrupt; try to soften what you say. Sprinkle your conversation with "please" and "thank-you." Never walk up to a box office and say "TWO!" Say, "May I have two tickets, please?"

- When forced to send food back in a restaurant, try to make it sound like it was your fault. Never say, "This steak is raw!" Say, "Ma'am, I know I'm peculiar about my steaks, but if you'd ask that old boy in the kitchen to throw this back on the fire for a minute, I'd dance at your wedding." This way nobody is mad and you get your steak the way you like it.

- Never accuse a Southerner of still fighting the War between the States. It did not turn out so well the first time and no Southerner I know wants to try again.

I guess what all of these suggestions are meant to do is to tell you not to call attention to yourself. The average Southern child is taught from birth never to do anything to call attention.

Above all, remember that if you act like somebody, folks will treat you like you're somebody.

MANNERS &
★ MORES ★

★ HOME REMEDIES ★

Home remedies are big in the South. The average Southerner will not go to a doctor unless a body part has dropped off or the heart has failed to beat for more than twenty minutes.

We are taught from the cradle that the best remedy is a home remedy. We are taught that doctor bills are only for the rich and those covered by worker's compensation.

When a Southerner gets sick, the first line of defense is food. In the way, way back of our memory, we hear our mama's voice saying, "Eat this, sugar . . . it will make you feel better."

Once, when I was about nine years old, I got a fishbone hung in my throat. No doctor, no ambulance, no dialing 911. They fed me a banana and two pieces of white bread. When I complained that I had swallowed the fishbone, but it felt like my throat had been scratched in the process, my mother said, "We'll just swab it out with some kerosene on a rag and you'll be good as new." I immediately assured her that my throat was really not scratched; it was only my imagination.

Kerosene is still widely used. If you should step on a nail rusty enough to kill a fence post, the remedy is to pour kerosene into the open wound. It is also used for a toothache. Yes sir! A little kerosene on a piece of cotton pressed against the gum will make your entire mouth taste like a BP station.

Practicing medicine at home was one of my sainted mother's special talents. She watched me like a mother hen, and at the first sign of something she deemed not quite normal, she would spring into action. When I was a child, I always felt that my mother had a less than wholesome interest in bowel habits. I believed then, as I do now, that my bodily functions should be between me and my Creator. My mother, on the other hand, was convinced that total health and happiness were the result of regular bowel habits.

It always started the same way. She would go into the bathroom after I had left and say, "It smells bad in here."

"It's supposed to smell bad, Mama; I just went to the bathroom in there."

"No, no," she would say. "You've got to have

some medicine, and I mean right now."

I knew what was coming, so I would plead my case: "Mama, it's supposed to smell bad. If you go to the bathroom and it doesn't smell bad, then you need medicine."

My arguments never changed her mind. Just before bedtime, she would come at me with a bottle of calomel. I only know two things about calomel: one, it tasted horrible, and, two, it tasted horrible. The old wives' tale about calomel was that if you took it and then got wet, it would make you a cripple, but I could never convince my mother that it was dangerous.

My mother tried everything possible to hide the wretched taste of that wretched medicine. One time, she put it in orange juice, and for many years I couldn't stand to be in the same room with a glass of orange juice.

The bouts we had over calomel were classic. She would try anything to get me to take it. She would try bribery: "If you take this like a good boy, I'll get you some ice cream." She would try to play on my sympathy: "I've worked hard all day; please take this so we can all go to bed and get some rest." She would try the old guilt trip: "If you loved me like you're supposed to, you'd take this for me." Then she would try the method that worked every time: "Okay young man, I've had about enough of this foolishness. You take this now or I'm going to wear you out!"

That always worked. It worked because my mother never bluffed. If she told you she was going to do something, she generally delivered.

In the years before penicillin and the sulfa drugs, the Southern wonder drug was Vicks salve. No home could hope for its residents to long survive if the medicine cabinet did not contain a large jar of Vicks. If you had a chest cold, it was rubbed all over your chest. Then you put on the top to your BVDs and slept under about three blankets. By morning your chest cold was supposed to be better, and many times it was. If you had a head cold, a big glob of Vicks was dropped into a pot of boiling water. You then were made to lean directly over the boiling water with a towel draped over your head, thus trapping the life-saving fumes under the towel where you were breathing and not diminishing their effectiveness with any fresh air. My mother would keep me in that position until my knees started to buckle and it was evident to all concerned that I was only seconds away from "death by Vicks." She would then take the towel away, look me right in my little bloodshot eyes and say, "Now, don't you feel a lot better?" I knew what was good for me, so I would fake a weak little smile and say, "Yes ma'am, a lot better." If I gave any other response, I knew that I would be going right back under that towel.

If, God forbid, I ever had a sore throat and the bad judgment to mention it, I was forced to swallow a spoonful of Vicks. I can remember to this day that it tasted exactly like a spoonful of 40-weight motor oil.

If, by any chance, the Vicks plan did not work, there was a last-resort cold remedy. I mean, of course, the mustard plaster. There were two types of mustard plasters. The first was the homemade variety. My grandmother made them herself in the kitchen. I don't know what it was made of, but I remember that it was yellow and smelled bad enough to make a buzzard sick. Again, you had to sleep in a wool BVD top in order to make this torture work. When you woke up in the morning (IF you woke up in the morning) the entire room smelled like you had been raising goats. It took about three soaking, scrubbing baths before you smelled like a human being again.

The second type of mustard plaster was the one that came from Glover's Pharmacy. It was adhesive and stuck to your chest sort of like a postage stamp. It didn't smell particularly bad and sleeping was relatively easy with it stuck to your chest. The horror of the store-bought mustard plaster, however, came with the rising sun when you had to face the certain reality that it was time for your mother to rip the thing from your cowardly, quivering chest.

When she came into the room, she would say, "Time to take that nasty mustard plaster off my baby's chest."

"Do it easy," I would plead.

"The faster I take it off," she would say, "the less it will hurt. You don't have any hair on your chest, so it will only hurt for a second."

She would then take the edge of the mustard plaster between her thumb and index finger. This was my cue to squeeze my eyes shut and say a silent prayer that the Lord would help me through this. Then, suddenly and with no warning, she would rip the mustard plaster savagely from my chest in one lightning-fast movement. The sound was like a cat being torn in two. It was over quickly, but I remember thinking, "My God, she's torn my nipples off. I'm only seven years old and must face the rest of my life with a nippleless chest. Dear Lord, I can never be a lifeguard." I was devastated. The vision of a slick-chested future loomed in front of me.

Then came the inevitable question, "Now, that wasn't so bad, was it?" I was worried about being a double nipple amputee, and there my mother was sitting on the side of the bed smiling. I would rather have lost both legs. I knew I could get wooden legs. I also knew that in the history of medical science, there was not a single case of anyone being fitted for artificial nipples. Words cannot express the relief I felt when I reached down and felt both nipples in place—raw and burning, but nonetheless in place.

My mother and grandmother were the home remedy experts of their day. They were absolutely convinced that any malady or sickness that struck the family could be cured with one record-setting bowel movement. It was to this end that I became the unwilling guinea pig for every laxative known to medical science. They thought that if they could disguise a laxative as chocolate, I would never know the difference. They told me that Ex-Lax was just like a Hershey bar. I remember thinking, "If it's just like a Hershey bar, how come you can't get it with almonds? And if it tastes so good, how come they ain't eatin' one?"

The same was true of Feenamint. They told me it was like a Chiclet. To this day, I won't chew Chiclets because they taste like Feenamint.

I will never forget Carter's Little Liver Pills. I don't know what they did for your liver, but I do remember for a BB-sized pill, they sure made you spend a lot of time in the bathroom.

Castor oil was too vile to even talk about. I'm not sure what its medical properties were, but it tasted so bad that I'm sure to this day my castor is well oiled.

Milk of magnesia tasted so bad that my mother wouldn't even give it to me. But that didn't stop my grandmother from giving it to me once. It tasted like a mixture of sour milk and camel sweat. I would rather die alone and friendless in the gutter than ever take it again.

666 was supposed to cure anything from baldness to brain tumors, but mostly it turned stomachs. I remember watching the faces of the grown-ups as they took a spoonful. Their mouths drew up tighter than panty-hose on Shelley Winters. I made a promise to myself that if they ever tried to make me take it, I would hang myself.

There was one cure that was many times worse than anything that could possibly be wrong with the human body. I refer, of course, to the dreaded enema. Even as a small child, I knew that God did not want me to have an enema. I had been taught in Sunday school that he was a just and loving God; besides, he didn't even do that to the Devil.

I guess we can sum up this chapter by saying that in the north, mothers thought that "an apple a day will keep the doctor away." Southern mothers, on the other hand, were convinced that "a laxative a week will make you hit your peak."

LIES TOLD SOUTHERN
★ CHILDREN ★

I was told from the time I was a little tyke that there are two kinds of lies. There were black lies that were meant to deceive and hurt other people. And there were white lies that were supposed to help people or spare their feelings.

If you told black lies, chances were about 70-30 that you would go to Hell when you died; on the other hand, white lies were not written against your name in God's scorebook.

But in looking back, it seems to me that there is a third kind of lie—the kind told to Southern children. The adults telling these lies no doubt considered them white, since they were intended to encourage proper conduct, but from the children's point of view . . . well, I'm not so sure. Let's look at some of the more common lies told to Southern children.

- Soap Sally: The standard lie started out, "If you're bad, Soap Sally will get you." Then it was explained that Soap Sally was an evil old woman who looked something like the witch in Snow White. She roamed the South with a croaker sack, looking for bad boys and girls. When she found one, she put the child in her sack, took it to her shack in the woods and made soap out of it. The police were not called and there was no investigation. Their disappearance was explained by saying, "Soap Sally got 'em."

- The snapping turtle: Every little boy in the South knew that if you were foolish enough to be bitten by a snapping turtle, you could be in serious trouble. The lie told us was that once a snapping turtle bit you, he would hang on until it thundered—no matter what. You could kill him and cut his head off and still he would hang on till the thunder came. I may have been just a little boy at the time, but it was easy to figure out that sometimes it would go for weeks without thunder. I had a horrible mental picture of going to Sunday school with a snapping turtle dangling from my index finger. I could just hear the taunts of the other children, "Look at that little boy. He must be a dumb ass. He was playing with a snapping turtle." I could see myself lying in bed at night with my turtle beside me holding on for dear life. I could hear my prayers: "God bless my mother and all my family, and please, please, dear God, please, please, please let it thunder soon."

- Cramps: We were told that if you went swimming within an hour of eating, you would get a cramp and drown. My black friend Junebug gave me a life-saving tip that was also a lie. He told me that if I would pee down my leg before going swimming in the wash hole, I would not get cramps. I must confess that I never heeded his advice, because I felt then, just as I feel now, that I would rather get cramps and drown than to pee on myself. I told Junebug that, and he said, "Okay . . . but if you get a cramp and drown, don't come complaining to me."

- Stunted growth: I can only assume that all Southern children wanted to be tall. I base that assumption on the fact that if we had any bad habits, we were told they would stunt our growth. I was convinced that one puff of rabbit tobacco would take about a foot off my ultimate size. We were told that all jockeys were two-pack-a-day men, but that cowboys never smoked.

- Masturbation: I don't know of any Southern child that ever discussed masturbation with his parents. It was just not done. Parents assumed that if they didn't mention it, it did not exist.

  The lies told about the dire consequences of masturbation came from older boys, though I am convinced that, originally, they came from grownups. The most common of all anti-masturbation lies was that it caused pimples. Nobody wanted pimples, but we all knew that somewhere there was a factory making Noxema.

  Some of the other effects, however, were not so easily remedied. It was said to be common scientific knowledge that excessive masturbation would cause hair to grow on the palm of your hand. In my young mind, I could only imagine the shame that would follow you through your lifetime if you were walking the streets of America with a hairy palm. Everyone you met on life's highways would know that you were nothing but a puddin-pullin' degenerate . . . girls would know, the preacher would know, and, God forbid, your mama would know. Could even a Southern mother love a hairy-palmed son?

If the pimples and hairy palms were not enough to keep us on the narrow path, think about this. We were assured that excessive masturbation would cause blindness. My heart went out to the blind people of the world even though I figured they had a few happy years before Mother Nature played her dirty trick. When I was about eleven years old, somebody told me about a man who had been blind since he was three. My only comment was, "WOW!" The lie about masturbation causing blindness gave rise to the popular joke: when the little boy was told that it would make him go blind, his question was, "Can I just do it until I need glasses?"

Whenever my mother would catch me doing something outside of her rules, I would ask, "How did you know?" She would smile and say, "A little bird told me." I don't guess I was too bright because for a long, long time, I was convinced that my mother had a close friendship with a stool-pigeon bird. The fact of the matter was that she was smarter than me, but before I realized that, I sure hated that little bird.

★ SOUTHERN SEX ★

I'm always amused when I read books and see movies about sex in the Deep South. You know the ones: beautiful women, handsome men, living in white-columned homes and having sex with everybody from the gardener to the chief of police. Yes sir, if we believe our writers and filmmakers, we would believe that Southern men and women rarely stand upright.

Well, it just ain't so. In the South of my teenaged years, not only was sex not free and easy, it was almost non-existent. It's not that we didn't try. And it's not that we didn't give it lots of thought; as a matter of fact, starting at about age fourteen, we thought of little else.

The older boys told us lies about their sexual exploits. We believed their lies because, more than anything else on earth, we wanted to believe them. They lied to us about how to make a girl "hot," and then, having convinced us that we could accomplish that task, went on to lie about the pure delight that was sure to follow. The heating method that seemed to enjoy the most popularity was putting cigarette ashes into a girl's Coke. It was common knowledge that this little trick would have any teenage girl "all over you." I had never had a girl all over me, but the implications were clear, and it was a prospect that certainly appealed to my teenage mind.

But there was a serious drawback to the old ashes-in-the-Coke method. None of us smoked. We were, therefore, doomed to failure before we started.

We were also told wild, outrageous tales about something called Spanish Fly. None of us had ever seen any, of course, and we didn't know if it was a powder, a pill, or an insect. We heard that it was something that vets gave to horses to "put them in the mood," so it made sense that if it would make a great big old horse amorous, it should certainly cause a teenage girl to attack the nearest teenage boy. But since we didn't know what Spanish Fly was, or how to get it, we could only fantasize that someday we might be fortunate enough to run into somebody selling this most wonderful potion. Needless to say, it never happened.

I don't know where we first heard it, but it was common knowledge among all teenage Southern boys that if you blew into a girl's ear, within a matter of seconds she would be "all over you." I tried it once with a young girl that I had talked into going to the movie with me. When I was sure no one would notice, I took a deep breath and blew long and softly into her ear. She turned and looked right into my sex-starved eyes. I remember thinking, what will I do if she starts to tear her clothes off right here in the movie? Finally, she spoke in a whisper: "What are you doing?"

That was the last response I was expecting. Embarrassed, I said, "I was blowing in your ear."

Unsmiling, she asked, "Why were you blowing in my ear?"

"I don't know," I stammered.

"Do you often blow into people's ears?"

"No," I said, "I swear to God this is my first ear."

"Well, stop it," she said, "It's stupid."

During the rest of the movie, I gave serious consideration to becoming a priest. That is no small decision for a fourteen-year-old Presbyterian.

My friend Herman was an inspiration to us all in those days. He didn't have any better luck with the fairer sex than we did, but he devoted his every waking moment to the pursuit thereof. He started using aftershave about three years before he started shaving.

One day, I saw him in the lobby of the movie holding hands with a girl. When she excused herself to go to the rest room, I asked, "Herman, what's that smell?"

"Old Spice" he said. "Man, if this don't turn her on, she ain't got no switches."

After the movie, Herman walked her outside where she got into a car with her mother, drove away and left poor Herman standing there on the curb. I remember thinking, "There goes a 98-cent bottle of Old Spice down the drain."

When we were about fifteen, we discovered a wonderful thing—a teenage girl who was as interested in learning about sex as we were. I lived in mortal fear that her daddy would find out about his daughter's horizontal activities and kill the boys involved. That same fear exists to this day, so I'll just refer to her as Mabel.

She was not a beautiful girl, but she was attractive and had what we all considered to be a wonderful, giving attitude. She was well dressed when she was dressed at all, and she gave new meaning to the word "next."

I don't know what ever happened to Mabel. I heard one time that she had married a soldier and moved away. I hope wherever she is that she realizes we never considered her a tart. Far from it. We always considered her the Johnny Appleseed of Sex.

Today the term sexual revolution is thrown

around quite a bit. But in my teenage years there were few skirmishes, no battles, and certainly no revolution. We would never "go all the way" with our steadies. We were taught that these girls were to be respected. If we were going to get lucky it was going to have to be with a girl that we didn't care much about. That idea seemed to keep us relatively pure.

I think, however, the thing that slowed down our sexual activity was that in a small town, you knew most of the girls' parents. You went to church with them. You were in Boy Scouts with their brothers.

It's hard to explain, but it just didn't seem like the thing to do. Nonetheless, we didn't feel deprived. Mabel took care of that.

The next time you see a movie or read a book about lust in the Deep South, think about my boyhood friend Herman . . . alone and reeking of Old Spice aftershave.

★ SOUTHERN DRIVERS ★

Southern drivers are, by far, the best in the world. If you doubt this ultimate truth, ask yourself this question: When you hear Richard Petty, Bill Elliott, or Cale* Yarbrough speak, do you pick up even a trace of a Boston accent? The answer is not "No," it's "Naw." Mr. Petty is from Randleman, North Carolina, Mr. Elliott is a native of Dawsonville, Georgia, and Cale Yarbrough hails from Timmonsville, South Carolina.

The reason I bring up the driving thing is because anytime there is ice or snow on the streets, my yankee friends like to say, "You people just don't know how to drive on ice or snow." (I really hate it when they call me "you people." I'm not "you people"; they are, by God, "you people.")

Most Southern people learned how to drive on slick, muddy, red-clay roads. Once you

---

* There has never been a yankee named Cale.

52

drive on a muddy Georgia road, ice and snow are child's play. I believe if Admiral Byrd had been from Ty Ty, Georgia, he would have driven to the North Pole and not run those poor dogs dang near to death.

There are many differences between northern and Southern drivers. Let's start with the most obvious. Southern drivers rarely shoot their fellow motorists. In the South, we find it more satisfying to drag the offender from his car and beat him senseless; besides, we like to save our ammunition for road signs.

I have a friend who is a giant of a man. He is 6'5" and on an average day will make a scale beg for mercy under his 275 pounds. He is a man of great good humor (thank goodness). The only flaw I have ever been able to find in his personality is the fact that he never gets a little mad. On the rare occasions that he is irritated, he loses all self-control.

On one such occasion, he had stopped for a red light when his car went dead. The light changed to green, and a motorist behind him in a little MG convertible started to blow his horn and scream at my large friend. When the Big Man realized that some of the obscenities contained unflattering references to his Mama, he jumped from his car and charged the tiny convertible. Noting that my friend was as big as a telephone booth, the other driver quickly rolled up his window and locked the door. This only served to anger the Big Man further. When it became apparent to him that he was unable to tear the MG's door from its hinges, he grabbed the convertible top, pulled it away from its moorings on the windshield, and punched the incredulous horn-blower in the face.

In the South, of course, blowing one's horn is considered common, simply unthinkable by anyone of good manners and breeding.

The other big difference between northern and Southern drivers is the use of blinker signals. Northern drivers not only use them to indicate a turn; they use them to warn that they are changing lanes. I have no explanation for this habit except that, perhaps, northern drivers use their blinkers and Southern drivers pay attention.

Pickup trucks in the South are much more than a mode of transportation. They are part of Southern culture and generally are treated with tender loving care.

Gun racks are not considered optional equipment. The theory is if you're not going to have a gun rack, you might as well be driving a sedan. The only time a real Southern driver would carry a gun in his gun rack, however, is during deer season; any other time, his peers would assume he was "showing out."

Gun racks should never be used to hold

umbrellas, though. Any Southern pickup owner who would put an umbrella in a gun rack would immediately have his sexuality called into question.

Whenever possible, Southern pickups are purchased with a floorboard stick shift. Young ladies dating a pickup owner always sit in the middle of the seat. The theory is a simple one, "If she is old enough to date, she is old enough to shift gears."

★ COURTING ★

There is a vast difference in northern courting and Southern courting.

In the north, if you take your true love out, you figure on no less than a five-course dinner complete with candlelight, flowers, and a sissy in the background playing "Three Coins in the Fountain" on the violin.

In the South, you spray-paint her name on a bridge abutment.

★ HOOVER DAYS ★

In the South, the Great Depression was—and is—called simply "Hoover Days." I grew up thinking that President Hoover, with malice afore-thought, had teamed with the rest of the Republicans and caused the Depression. In talk-ing to the old-timers about it, I was never able to tell if they enjoyed it or were just proud that they had survived those dark days. I say this because, even to this day, they love to talk about it. Describing just how poor they were seems to have stimulated their creative facul-ties:

> "We were so poor, the only thing I got for Christmas was a walnut."

> "Times were so hard, the Chattahoochee River only ran three times a week."

"Most folks were so poor they couldn't afford to give their children middle names."

"Our mule ate a heap better than we did."

"We ate so much possum that my nose started to turn pink."

"The only thing we had to eat on a regular basis was cathead biscuits and syrup. If we didn't make a good crop, we ate cathead biscuits and lard."

"The first piece of loaf bread I ever seen blowed off the back of a CCC truck."

"The first pair of new shoes I ever had was when I went into the Army."

"We had to eat a lot of rabbit. We didn't have no shotguns so we had to kill 'em any way we could. The worst whippin' I ever got was the time my mama gave me three rocks and I didn't bring home but two rabbits."

"Only rich people could afford cardboard

to put in their shoes."

"Mama would have given us soup-bowl haircuts, but we didn't have no soup bowls."

The Hoover Days stories go on and on. If President Hoover was the villain of those days, President Roosevelt was a bigger hero than Robert E. Lee. F.D.R. was everybody's hero in the Deep South. You just never heard one word against him.

I was too young to understand a lot about politics, but I had heard all the grown-ups talk about what he had done for the country by whippin' Hoover and stopping the Depression. I grew up thinking that being a Republican was worse than being a child molester. I didn't know anyone who had a civil word to say about the Grand Old Party, but I had heard the grown-ups talk about Wendell Wilkie, and it was common knowledge that if he beat President Roosevelt, we'd be living in caves in less than thirty days.

We stayed up late that election night and listened to the returns come in on the radio. Then we got up early to see if it was official. It was . . . our beloved president had beaten Wilkie like he had stolen a government check. The same was true when Tom Dewey had the gall to run against "our president." I remember the things the old men used to say about Dewey:

"Look at that little weasel. He's got enough oil in his hair to grease a Greyhound bus bumper to bumper."

"You can just look at him and tell he's a crook, can't you?"

"Yeah, and not only that, he looks right funny out of his eyes."

I couldn't for the life of me figure out how any politician in his right mind could have the nerve to run against F.D.R. You could just listen to him on the radio and know that he was a great man. Didn't he make the Depression go away? Didn't he tell the Japanese and Germans that he was going to wear 'em out? Didn't he come to Georgia on a regular basis? Yes sir, in the Deep South President Roosevelt was a true hero to children and grown-ups alike. Funny thing—none of the grown-ups liked Eleanor Roosevelt, but they didn't talk bad about her much because of their respect for the president.

I think that the Depression hurt less in the South than in the rest of the country. We were already poor, and the boll weevil came along and just about did in the Southern economy. We were still numb from that when the Hoover Days fell on the country like a load of cord wood.

Southerners, by their very nature, are politically conservative. They believe that when you have a family, it's your job to take care of them, and that includes your mama and daddy. We look to each other for help long before we look to the government.

I guess when the old folks look back and talk with pride about making it through the Hoover Days, it's not that they enjoyed them. It's that they survived those tough times with their dignity intact.

★ COMPANY'S COMING ★

In the South, when relatives come for an overnight visit, they never stay at a hotel. Good manners and Southern breeding require that they stay at your house, no matter how crowded it gets.

My grandmother and grandfather came to Atlanta from the Carolinas around the turn of the century, a young couple eager to escape the cotton mills and to start a new and better life. Their brothers and sisters stayed in the Carolinas but would come to visit us from time to time.

We never seemed to have much notice when the hungry hoard was coming. They never called in advance, since in those days you didn't make long-distance calls frivolously. They would call us from the north side of town to let us know they were on their way. It never seemed to bother my grandmother. Her main concern was that she had enough for them to eat.

She would hang up the phone and say, "Okay . . . we've all got to pitch in. Brother and his family will be here in a couple of hours, and after that long trip from Rock Hill they're gonna be hungry."

She would then go into the back yard with her apron full of chicken feed, throw some on the ground and say in a soft, soothing voice, "Chick, chick, chickie babe. Chick, chick, chickie babe." The chickens would gather at her feet, clucking and pecking up the feed, and the whole time my grandmother was shopping for the nicest, fattest fryers. Once she had made her decision, her right hand would shoot out like a cobra and grab a chicken. In a split second its neck was wrung, and it was flopping around on the ground like a mortally wounded breakdancer.

She kept right on shopping: "Chick, chick, chickie babe." In short order there were three or four chickens on the ground, their souls already departed and their earthly remains on the way to the big black frying pan.

Inside the house, my mother and my aunts were cleaning and scrubbing and putting fresh sheets on all the beds. It was an unwritten law that company got the pick of the beds, and we slept on whatever beds were left or on pallets on the floor.

When Uncle John and his family arrived, Mama was only minutes away from putting supper on the table. Uncle John would invariably say, "Bessie, you shouldn't have gone to so much trouble," and Mama would answer, "It's nothing special, John, nothing special."

I would be off in the corner watching and listening. I remember thinking, "Nothing special?! God almighty!" The woman had killed a yard full of chickens, fixed five different vegetables, plus banana pudding. If she had fixed any more, she would've had to buy a bigger table. I have heard all my life about how the children always ate after the adults. Little Jimmy Dickens even did a song about it called "Take an Old Cold Tater and Wait." But this was never the case at our house. The children ate first. When we had had our fill, the plates were cleaned, and only then did the grown-ups eat. There was always plenty, anyway; after the children got through, you could hardly tell any food was gone. I heard Mama say time after time, "These babies need their nourishment. And besides, ain't an adult here that it would hurt to miss a meal." Of course, nobody ever missed a meal.

After supper, we'd all go into the parlor, and the snapshots would be brought out. "Lawdy! I can't believe that child is grown and married." "Don't he look precious with his cap and gown.

I betcha he could make a doctor." "John, I never seen so many good pictures. You must keep a Kodak in your hands all the time."

When it was bedtime, we found our pallets and settled in for the night. For a while, there was a lot of whispering and giggling among the children, but then a grown-up would say, "You children hush. It's time you were asleep. Get quiet now. Say your prayers and go to sleep." In a few days, the relatives would all pack up and go back to Rock Hill. It was crowded and hectic, but even after all these years I remember mostly how much fun it was.

★ YANKEE-WATCHING ★

Life in the rural South can be boring at times. In a small town, not much is open on Sunday, and you often have only three options to fight the tedium: you can watch the water tank leak; you can wax your yo-yo string; or you can go to the Stuckey's out on the highway and do some yankee-watching.

I have never been able to understand the mind-set of northern tourists. If you judge by the way they dress, you can only assume that they think they're invisible. Let's talk about the women first.

About fifty percent of the time, the women have their hair up in curlers. Is it possible that they drive all the way from Michigan to Florida with their hair up in these pink ugly things? They like to wear plaids and stripes together. It is one of their rules to be sure that none of the colors make any pretense of matching. They insist on wearing shorts with no regard whatsoever to the fact that their varicose veins make their legs look like an aerial photograph of the Los Angeles freeway system. I guess their strangest habit is wearing sandals with white socks. I wonder why they do that.

The men also wear shorts, and some also wear sandals with socks, but for the most part they seem to prefer Wingtips with over-the-calf black socks. The men all want to grow beards on their vacation, and by the time they get to south Georgia, they have a two-day stubble. On any given Sunday in the summer, every Stuckey's in the South looks like it's convening a Gabby Hayes look-alike contest.

The children all wear flipflops, and they all have on t-shirts that read "I (heart) New York" or "I (heart) Detroit." Apparently some northern law requires that all children carry radios. The most fun is to listen to their comments. You don't have to eavesdrop because for some strange reason they all talk louder than we do. You hear things like:

"Don't put that in your mouth. You don't know where it's been."

"Raymond, are you sure you locked the car?"

"Did you see that man staring at my legs?" (No doubt someone marveling at the varicose veins.)

"Mommie, this ham is too salty."

"Christamighty."

"I'd like a tongue sandwich and an order of fries."

"Does Jimmy Carter ever stop here?"

"Scumbag."

"Do you sell cream sodas?"

"Mama, there is a machine in the toilet that sells French ticklers."

"What the hell is a grit?"

"No, Robbie, I will not pay $12.95 for a stuffed baby crocodile."

I'm sure that when Southern tourists go up north for a vacation we do things that they don't understand. We must seem just as funny to them as they seem to us . . . NAAAAAA.

★ SOUTHERN ★ ACCENTS

★ A SOUTHERN ★ GLOSSARY

I have never read a book about the South that didn't have a so-called dictionary of Southern words. They are pretty much the same: *Y'all, dawg, Gawd* and *Jawga.* I have always felt that the beauty of the way native Southerners speak is in their expressive words and phrases. Let's explore some of these as well as their meanings:

- "I ain't got no dog in that fight" means "That is none of my business."

- "That dog won't hunt" means "That is a bad or unworkable plan."

- "He is a right hard dog to keep under the porch" means that the man in question is either a womanizer or a drunk. In some cases he could also be a womanizing drunk.

- "He is about a half-bubble out of plumb" describes the kind of person who could not find his own rear end with a ten-man working party.

- "The cheese has slipped off his cracker" means "He was rational yesterday, but seems to have lost touch with reality." This person probably said something like "Read my lips, no new taxes" or "I tried pot once but didn't inhale."

- "Laid up in bed" means one of two things. It could mean someone is ill, as in "Lou's got the flu and is laid up in bed." It could also mean that someone is committing adultery, as in "He is laid up in bed with an old woman."

- "Lay-about" describes a person who's too lazy to do anything but lay around the house and watch "Bonanza" reruns. For example, "Your common garden-variety lay-about did not even notice the Great Depression. He would not work if he had a job with nothing to do and a helper. He is a complete outcast and is only loved by the good old girl that supports him."

- "Take drunk" means to get drunk completely by accident: "He was getting ready for work, had one Budweiser just to cool off, and the next thing he remembers, he was having a conversation with a door hinge." The correct usage of the phrase is "John had planned to go to work, but he took drunk."

- "Puny" indicates a degree of sickness. When you are "puny" you are able to sit up and take nourishment, but unable to go to work.

- "No count" is a term that receives wide usage in the South. As in: "The store had tomatoes, but they wasn't no count." Or, "He has plenty of money, but he ain't no count." "The truck only has 15,000 miles on it, but it ain't no count." To set the record straight, "no account" means the same thing as "no count," but is used primarily by high school graduates.

- "Cold as a witch's tit" means "very cold." I don't know where this expression came from, but I would like to meet the man who did the initial research.

- "Cool as the center seed of a cucumber" is used to describe a person who handles pressure well.

- "He knows as much about that as a hog knows about Sunday" means "He's totally ignorant about the subject and should hush."

- "Preaching to the choir" means explaining something to someone who knows more about the subject than you do.

- "Sorry" can be confusing. In the north when someone is sorry, it means he feels a sense of sorrow, as in "I'm sorry the hogs ate your little brother." In the South, however, it can mean something entirely different. It has nothing to do with sorrow, but instead indicates a character flaw, as in "He is too sorry to scratch. He is one sorry teenager." When someone in the South is said to be sorry, it can also be assumed that he is no count, shiftless and, to one degree or another, a lay-about.

- "Useless as tits on a boar hog" is self-explanatory, and if you don't understand it, in all likelihood, you shoplifted this book.

- "Broke bad" means that things went wrong, very wrong. Examples: "Georgia was ahead at the half, then it broke bad." Or, "They had twelve happy years together, then it broke bad." Or, "They were happy together until he set fire to her leg . . . her daddy came over, and it broke bad."

- "Slack-eyed" is a medical diagnosis and means the patient is near death, as in "Don't waste the adrenalin on him, Doc, he's done got slack-eyed."

- "Don't that take the rag off the bush" means "Isn't that amazing." This expression was first used when Jefferson Davis found out that Sherman had burned Atlanta, hung a left and was headed for Savannah.

- "He can run like a scalded dog" means "He can flat run." The only way you can get the full impact of this phrase, however, is to be willing to scald your dog. This phrase can be used interchangeably with "run like a wild Indian going to the outhouse." (The politically correct version, "run like a native American going to the bathroom," seems to lose something.)

- "The finest woman who ever sewed for the Baptists" describes the woman who is the pillar of the community and is held in the utmost esteem by everyone who knows her. She is active in no less than three charities and has a son who is a missionary in Perth Amboy, Michigan.

- "Sorry as gully dirt" means "third-degree sorry." Like gully dirt, this person is unable and unwilling to produce anything.

- "Best cook I ever ate behind" is a self-explanatory compliment and is only used when referring to one's mother or wife. It would be considered very bad form to offer this compliment to a Waffle House cook.

- "Don't worry about the mule going blind, just load the wagon" means "Don't sweat the small stuff. Put your attention on the large tasks and the small ones will take care of themselves." (Besides, a blind mule can pull as heavy a load as one with 20/20 vision.)

- "You can't tell a man about his own mule" means "You are trying to tell somebody something he already knows."

- "Come see us." Actually, the very last thing this means is "come see us." It is simply the Southerner's way of saying goodbye, and is, by no stretch of the language, to be considered an invitation.

- "It's comin' up a cloud" means "It is about to rain."

- "A gully washer" means "a heavy rain."

- "A frog strangler" means "a hell of a rain."

- "Loop-legged" denotes an advanced state of drunkenness, as in "By eleven o'clock he had done got loop-legged, and by midnight he was so drunk he thought he was invisible, bullet-proof, and out of debt."

- "Fixin" means "preparing to do something," as in "I'm fixin' to go to town" or "I'm fixin' to go to bed." It can also mean "I am about to start cooking," as in "I'm fixin' to fix dinner."

- "Gravy-sucking pig" is a Southern insult that is reserved for a no-count, shiftless, sorry-as-gully-dirt lay-about. The only other thing left to say after you have called someone a gravy-sucking pig is to remind him that in all likelihood, his mama wears a flea collar.

- "Constipated." When you say that someone is constipated, it has nothing to do with the action in his colon. It has to do with his outlook on life, the way he holds his lips together and rarely smiles.

★ TWO LANGUAGES ★ SEPARATED BY THE MASON DIXON LINE

To shed a little further light on the Southern idiom, let's compare some of our terminology to that of our northern neighbors.

- We call them "sundecks"; they call them "fire escapes."

- They go to the shore; we go to the beach.

- They queue up; we stand in line.

- Sometimes they stand on line; we still stand in line.

- They take a shave; we just shave.

- They call it "the forest"; we call it

"the woods."

- They call it "the Golf of Mexico"; we call it "the Gulf of Mexico."

- They say, "That person is emaciated." We say, "He looks a little wormy."

- They say, "That food is very filling." We say, "It lays heavy on your chest."

- They say, "Watch it, fella." We say, "Excuse me."

- They say, "Would you give me a ride to the store?" We say, "Would you run me to the store?"

- After heavy exercise, they get sore; we get stove up.

- Their 7-11 employees say, "Have a nice day." Ours say, "Come back."

- They say, "My car has electrical problems." We say, "It ain't gettin' no fire."

- They argue; we fuss.

When my travels take me up north, it's

always a little surprising when someone offers me a soda, or a pop. I once asked why they refer to all soft drinks as "pop." I was told, "Because 'pop' is the sound they make when they are opened." It would seem to me that anyone with normal hearing, north or South, would know that when you open a soft drink they don't go "pop," they go "whoosh." It would, of course, make little or no sense to call one a "Whoosh." You could find yourself in real trouble if your girlfriend's father asked where you were taking his daughter and you said, "We're going out for a Whoosh."

I love the difference in the way we talk. I worry a lot about the fact that television is causing our Southern accent to sound more midwestern, or even northern. I read the other day that a school had opened up in Atlanta to help people lose their Southern accents. It's just another way to apologize for being Southern. Wouldn't it be sad if everybody in America sounded just like Roger Mudd?

★ SOUTHERN THREATS ★

I have traveled all over the fruited plain as a banquet speaker. I was for many years an insurance adjuster. I tell you this to make the point that, in my life, I have met and dealt with people from every walk of life, and I am convinced that Southerners make the best threats.

I have also learned that threats made by Southerners are usually empty threats and by their very nature would be impossible to carry out. You know, for example, if someone tells you that he is going to unscrew your belly button till your legs fall off, there is no medical way to do that. You also know, however, that you have displeased this person.

If someone tells you that he is going to "jerk a knot in your pucker string," it gets your attention . . . even if you never knew that you had a pucker string. Speaking for myself, I don't want a knot jerked into anything I have, including my pucker string.

Many Southern threats contain the word "snatch," as in "I'm going to snatch you bald-headed" or "I'm going to reach down your throat and snatch out your liver." While I don't believe it is possible to carry out either one of these threats, I wouldn't want to press my luck.

The threat every Southern child hears by the time he is three years old is "I'm going to wear you out." This threat traditionally comes from your mama. When you are a child, you don't really know at once what it means. If, however, you give it some thought, it boggles your little mind. You have never actually seen a human being worn out, but you know what your every-day play shoes look like when they are worn out. They are scuffed and cracked and full of holes. They are usually thrown in the back of your closet and forgotten about, where they stay, alone and ugly. When you think of it in those terms, being worn out is a serious threat and should certainly get the attention of any bright Southern child.

The same goes for any child who is told by his angry mother, "I'm going to slap you cross-eyed." When you are five or six years old, it seems perfectly logical that a grown-up could slap you cross-eyed. But I never worried much about this threat for two reasons: first, my mother almost never struck me, and second, if someone could slap you cross-eyed, it stands to reason that someone else could slap you uncross-eyed.

"Slap you silly" was another one that didn't bother me much. I knew that if someone ever slapped me silly, chances were good that, somewhere down the line, someone else would do me the favor of slapping me serious.

My boyhood friend Dee had a threat that he used every time he got into an argument with another twelve year old. Dee would say in a loud voice, "Oh yeah?! I'm going to hit your ass in the head with a rock." I never knew exactly what that meant, but I knew that I didn't want to be hit anywhere with a rock.

Let's list some of the memorable threats that you might hear in any argument in the South.

- "I'm going to knock you naked and hide your clothes." This threat not only holds the certainty of pain, but no Southerner worth a bowl of grits would want to be seen unclothed in public.

- "I'm going to hit you so hard your shirt will go up your back like a window shade." This threat would have been right at home in any Abbot and Costello movie.

- "I'm going to hit you so hard it will hurt your relatives."

- "I'm going to beat you like a red-headed stepchild." This threat was used mostly before red-headed stepchildren realized that they had civil rights.

- "I'm going to beat the living daylights out of you." This Southern threat never made any sense to anyone and was usually made by a witless mouthbreather.

- "I'm going to hit you so hard you'll starve to death before you quit bouncing."

- "If you don't shut up, I'm going to slap your mama." The clown who would make this threat was apparently too dumb to realize that my mama slapped back.

- "I'm going to beat you like a rented mule." This is a very creative threat. Anybody who ever had a mule knows that the temptation to beat it will occasionally rear its ugly head. Only a fool would risk hurting an expensive mule, but a rented mule is fair game.

- "I'm going to beat you like you stole a government check."

- "I'm going to kick you so hard you'll have to unzip your pants to eat."

It is a sad commentary, but there are many great Southern threats that are too obscene to put in a book that will be read by decent people. I have tried to clean up a couple of them to give you the idea:

- "One more word and I'm going to knock your weewee in the dirt."

- "I'm going to tear off your head and pee in your neck."

Let me repeat that most Southern threats are empty. They might be used to frighten or intimidate, but are generally our way of showing our creativity. There is one exception, however, that you should know about. If a Southerner ever makes one of the aforementioned threats and then screams "YEEEEE HA!" it would be advisable to leave the area at once.

★ SOUTHERN ★ OBSERVATIONS ON PHYSICAL IMPERFECTIONS

The Southern gift for expressive, descriptive language is also apparent in our way of noting the physical imperfections of others, as in the following:

- She is so bowlegged, she couldn't hem a hog up in a ditch.

- Their children were so ugly that when they made home movies, they hired stand-ins.

- Looks like her face caught fire and somebody beat it out with a shovel.

- He was so ugly, his mama had to tie

a pork chop around his neck to get the dogs to play with him.

- That old boy's ugly as homemade sin.

- She is ugly as a lard bucket full of armpits.

- He is so ugly he could make a freight train take a dirt road.

- She is ugly enough to knock a buzzard off a gut wagon.

- His nose is so big he could smoke a cigar in the shower.

- He'd make a gorilla gag.

- He's so skinny, he can get into a t-shirt from either end.

- That girl is so skinny that if she swallowed an olive, nine guys would leave town.

★ CUSSIN' ★

Cussin' down South is different. There is line of decency that is not crossed in mixed company. My friend Bo Whaley, the sage of Dublin, Georgia, summed it up when he told me that he never knew Jesus Christ was a cuss word until he moved up north. I will not give you examples of northern cussin'. If you have been to the picture show in the last few years, you are probably an expert on the subject.

Let's review the way Southern women cuss. The very first thing a little girl in the South hears from her mother is "Pretty is as pretty does." That means that no matter how much money you have spent on clothes, makeup, or your hair, one cuss word out of your well-made-up lips can make you as ugly as a bucketful of armpits. Southern women are allowed to say "shucks," "poop," "fiddle sticks," "fiddle-dee-dee," "fiddle faddle," "darn," "heck," "drat," "pshaw," "gosh darn," and "fudge." That's about it. They are never allowed to mention any body part, all of which are referred to as "you know what." As in: "If you don't leave my boyfriend alone, I'm going to beat your you know what."

Southern men, on the other hand, can be real trashmouths, but only if there are no ladies in the area. They use many of the cuss words that you hear up north, but they prefer native cussin' whenever possible. "Yo mama" is a favorite. It can be used in many ways. For example, if you wish to call someone a liar, you simply wait until he is finished his lie and say, "Yo mama." An effective variation would work as follows. If someone tells you that Auburn is going to whip Georgia on Saturday, your reply would be a simple "Yo mama is gonna beat Georgia."

Another favorite is "sumbitch," and it, too, can be meant in a variety of ways, depending upon the context:

- "I really miss that old sumbitch."

- "Boy! It is one hot sumbitch."

- "It rained like a sumbitch."

- "He can throw a baseball faster than a sumbitch."

- "I love her like a sumbitch."

- "It was cold as a sumbitch last night."

- "He's such a sumbitch, Mother Teresa once gave him the finger."

- "He is one ugly sumbitch."

There aren't many guidelines for native Southern cussin'. One, however, that bears mentioning is that you never include anyone's mama when you are cussin' him. It's hard to explain, but in the South "yo mama" and "sumbitch," as used above, are not considered to be an insult to one's mother. But if you ever cross the line and say something like "Yo mama wears a flea collar," you'd better have your Blue Cross paid up.

★ YOU ALL ★

Our New Southern friends have a lot of trouble with two little words: "You all." I guess the confusion started in Hollywood when somebody playing a Southern Belle in a movie referred to her boyfriend as "you all."

When used improperly, these two little words fall hard on Southern ears. To remedy the situation, my friend Betty M. Burks of Fayetteville, Georgia, put pen to paper and came up with this wonderful and educational poem.

Many thanks to Betty for sending it to me and allowing us to use it here.

YOU ALL

To all of you from other parts,
Both city folks and rural,
Please listen while I tell you that
The phrase "you all" is plural.

When we say, "You all must drop by,
Or we all shall be lonely,"
We mean a dozen folks perhaps,
And not one person only.

If I should say to Mr. Jones,
For instance, "You all's lazy,"
Or, "Will you all lend me a hand?"
He'd think that I was crazy.

Now if you'd be more sociable
And with us often mingle,
You'd find that on the native tongue
"You all" is never single.

Don't think I mean to criticize,
Or act as if I knew all:
But when we speak of one alone,
We all say "you" . . . like you all.

★ FAVORITE ★ FLAVORS

★ CORNBREAD ★

There was a time in the South when we said, "Cotton is king." This was before the boll weevil came along. Now there is not much doubt about who the new king is . . . cornbread. Golden brown, warm and wonderful; delicious with butter, buttermilk, or butterbeans. It was as much at home in President Carter's White House as it is in a lunch bucket in Spartanburg, South Carolina.

It is as Southern as a mint julep, as pure as a Bible verse, and as beautiful as a $700 mule. Every truly fine Southern cook knows how to make it, and there are literally hundreds of recipes for cornbread.

To the best of my knowledge, there is only one sure-fire test to tell if your cornbread is acceptable on a Southern table. If it tastes like your mama's, you are in for some good eatin'.

The only word of warning I would have is that

no matter what your recipe calls for, you must never, never, never put sugar in it. It makes it taste like cake and will brand you as an incompetent buffoon. There are documented cases of men being asked to resign from the Rotary Club after it became public knowledge that their wives put sugar in their cornbread.

I am one of the luckiest men on earth. My mother was a great cornbread cook, and my beautiful wife, Diane, can make cornbread with anybody that ever put on an apron. Here is the way my Diane makes her cornbread:

> 1 egg, beaten lightly
> 2 cups of cornmeal mix (if you're a
>   purist, buy plain cornmeal and add
>   your own baking powder and salt)
> 1 1/2 cups milk
> 2 tablespoons bacon grease (no substitutions)

Add all the wet ingredients to the cornmeal. Stir well. Preheat the oven to 400 degrees. Put another two tablespoons of bacon grease in your iron skillet and melt the grease in the oven. Take it out and roll the grease around the pan with a few crumpled paper towels. Pour the cornbread batter in and bake until it's nice and brown . . . 20 to 25 minutes.

Then, get ready for some fine, fine eating.

There are several ways to fix good cornbread—fried cornbread, Mexican cornbread, cracklin' . . . They are all great. This recipe is pretty much traditional; it will not only establish you as a good cook, but everyone will know you learned about cornbread at your Southern mama's knee.

★ BARBECUE ★

One of the great shocks of my life occurred on a visit to the north.

The friend I was staying with said, "We're going to barbecue tonight. Would that be all right with you?"

"All right?" I answered. "I not only love barbecue; I am considered somewhat of an authority in my beloved South."

When suppertime approached, I headed for the back yard to get a first-hand look at the pit, around which I was sure there would be several folks barbecuing a pig. There was no pit and, to my horror, no pig.

I found my friend in his carport cooking hamburgers and hot dogs on a charcoal grill.

"I thought you were going to barbecue," I said with a slight tear in my voice.

"What do you think I'm doing?" he asked.

I said, "You're cooking on the grill."

He laughed and said good-naturedly, "You dumb rebel, this *is* barbecuing."

I want you to get the picture. My friend thought cooking on the grill was barbecuing, and he was calling *me* dumb.

Of course, there's nothing you can do about yankee ignorance except laugh it off. Of much greater concern to me is what's happening here in the South. I'm afraid that we're losing our reverence for barbecue. In the not-too-distant past, we referred to barbecue places as barbecue joints. The name was a badge of honor.

One day, somebody got the idea of making barbecue joints more upscale. They cleaned them up and even painted them. They gave them cutesy names like "The Barbecue Kitchen." They even changed the spelling to Bar B Q. They added hamburgers and hot dogs to the menu. They paved the parking lots and added salad bars. They were allowed to open and operate with absolutely no regard for tradition.

In the vast number of cases, I am opposed to any type of government guidelines. In the case of barbecue, however, something must be done now. I have put together a list of guidelines that should be made law as soon as it can be pushed through congress. Once this legislation is enacted, hundreds of barbecue joints will start to spring up and we can restore barbecue to its rightful place as one of the four basic food groups.

Guidelines

1. Only barbecue pork can be served, not so-called barbecue beef. No hamburgers, no hot dogs. Pork and pork only.

2. There must be at least one religious slogan on the walls.

3. Painting of exterior and interior walls should be discouraged.

4. Waitresses only. Waiters may be permitted behind the counter only. All table service will be handled by women named Roxy and Hester.

5. Unsweetened iced tea will not be allowed.

6. No more than one word will be allowed as the name of the joint; i.e., Harold's, Mobley's, Porky's, Slope's, etc.

7. The owner must keep either a kitchen match or a toothpick hanging out of his mouth anytime he is on duty.

8. The bathrooms should be unfit for human beings and be out of order at least two days a week.

9. Tabasco sauce must be on every table.

10. When the waitress approaches the table, she must say either, "Can I hep you?" or "What's your's?"

11. Both mild and hot barbecue sauce must be offered.

Eleven very simple rules which, once made the law of the land, could change the world for the better.

★ BISCUITS ★

It's very difficult to explain to a non-Southerner just how important homemade biscuits are to the average Southern table. They are not only a part of our diet; they are part of our lives.

If you ever want to bring tears to a Southern man's eye, just get him talking about his mama's biscuits. He will enumerate their virtues—their lightness, fluffiness, flavor—with an eloquence usually reserved for Southern womanhood and the Confederate dead.

In many Southern homes, biscuits are served three meals a day. In addition, left-over breakfast biscuits are saved for children's after-school snacks.

Biscuits and gravy are considered a meal unto themselves. We have restaurants that serve only biscuits: steak biscuits, sausage biscuits, ham biscuits, bacon biscuits, and cheese biscuits.

We consider a slice of tomato in a biscuit to

be one of the great delicacies of life, and syrup and biscuit is to die for.

Southern biscuits come in all sizes, from small, two-bite ones to the wonderful cathead, so called because it is as big as a cat's head. It is rare to find two Southern cooks who have the same recipe, and as I have said before, the only true test to determine the quality of a biscuit is "does it taste like Mama's?" If the answer to that question is "yes," then all is well. If the answer is "no," then the marriage is doomed to end up in divorce court.

It would be easy to travel a hundred miles in any direction in the South and gather more than a thousand biscuit recipes that people swear by. The one offered here is my Diane's. It is the one I swear by.

It is a well-known Southern fact that true Deep South biscuits must be made with lard. We know that most medical experts agree that lard will kill you. We also know that some things are worth dying for:

2 cups sifted flour
2 teaspoons baking powder
1/4 teaspoon baking soda
3/4 teaspoon salt
1/4 cup lard
about 1 cup buttermilk

Heat the oven to 475 degrees. Sift together the flour, baking powder, salt, and soda. Cut in the lard until the mixture looks like coarse cornmeal. Stir in buttermilk with a fork until a soft dough forms. Knead and roll out onto a lightly floured board. Cut into desired thickness. Bake about ten minutes.

Your first bite will tell you that the best croissant ever baked pales beside a good Southern biscuit.

SOUTHERN FRIED
★ CHICKEN ★

Fried chicken in the South is much more than a kind of food. It is a trademark, a symbol. It is eaten with delight and gusto by the very rich and the very poor. It is looked upon with love and reverence by every race and religion. It is eaten by Baptists, Methodists, Presbyterians, Seventh Day Adventists, Christian Scientists, Catholics, Jews, and Walter Matthau fans. It is served at weddings, funerals, and Elvis sightings. It was eaten by Washington, Jefferson, Rhett Butler, and my cousin Doodle.

The love of fried chicken is common to all Southerners. Before I tell you the best way to make real Southern fried chicken, let me tell you how it is cooked up north. First, they soak it in buttermilk. Then they cover it with bread crumbs or some kind of batter. Then they fry it in about a half-inch of vegetable oil.

I am a very, very lucky man because my Diane is one of the best fried chicken cooks ever to light a stove. In our book *The Fat White Guy's Cookbook*, Diane explains the magic she uses in cooking her Southern fried chicken:

"You go to the store and buy five chicken breast halves. I skin them before I put them in the refrigerator. When I'm ready to use them, I take them out and wash them again. While they're still wet, I drop them individually into a plastic bag that has about two cups of flour, a few shakes of salt, and a generous amount of pepper. I put the coated chicken on a platter and leave it alone for 30 to 45 minutes. Leaving it alone is probably the most important step. When I come back, the chicken looks like it's been dipped in wallpaper paste. That's going to make the crisp "skin." Then I put two to three inches of vegetable oil in my big iron skillet and heat it on medium high until it sizzles when a speck of flour drops in. I brown the chicken quickly on both sides. Always turn the chicken with tongs, never with a fork. If you don't pierce the chicken, the juices stay in and the grease stays out. Finally, I turn the breasts meaty side down and cover the pan. Fry them slowly, covered, for 30 minutes. Drain on a paper towel."

I guess every family in the South has a special way to cook their chicken. I can only tell you that Diane's is my favorite and that it's so authentic it's hard to eat it without softly humming, "That's what I like about the South."

★ OLD-TIME ★
RELIGION

★ RELIGION ★ DOWN SOUTH

Religion in the South is practiced not only in the church. Many businesses are built on the fact that the proprietor is a practicing Christian. Once you have been assured that the businessman is indeed a good Christian, then you know that you can trust him and that his word is his bond.

Alas, if it were only true. The unhappy truth is that in the Southern Bible Belt many folks use religion to help them turn a buck, honest or otherwise. Such a man was the famous used car salesman, Lindley M. Aaron.

Lindley's life had been spent cheating people on used car deals. He was completely without conscience, and honesty was as foreign to him as Bosnia-Herzegovina.

Then, one day, Lindley announced that he had

found the Lord and that the remainder of his years would be spent selling used cars for Jesus. In an effort to attract other religious people to his used car lot, he ran the following ad in the local paper: "Uncle Lindley, the working man's friend. Your credit, brother and sister, is good with Uncle Lindley. Everybody rides . . . we finance anybody . . . drunks, ex-cons, out of work druggies, or wetbacks. Small downpayment and proof of church membership is all you need at Uncle Lindley's Bible-believing car lot."

The truth of the matter was that if you had the "small" downpayment, Lindley would waive the proof of church membership.

Lindley had a special formula for determining the downpayment on a used car. The downpayment was the value of the car plus ten percent. If, for example, you wanted a car that was actually worth $500, the downpayment was $550, and the monthly payment was whatever Uncle Lindley could talk you into. If you made the payments, Lindley was happy. If you missed a payment, he was even happier, because that meant he could repossess the car and sell it again. With the prospects of a repossession looming, he would smile and say, "Praise the Lord. I must rise up and smite this ingrate debtor directly in his pocketbook."

When the poor debtor objected to his car being repossessed, Lindley would begin preaching in a loud voice, "It's in the Book, brother! The Lord hates a whoremonger and a debt defaulter." The poor man would say, "I ain't no whoremonger," to which Lindley would reply, "And brother, when I leave here with my car, you will no longer be a loan defaulter. Praise the Lord! I have saved this poor wretch from the pits of burning Hell by repossessing this car; I have cleansed him of his sin of bad debt. Praise the Lord!"

Lindley's fortune soared. He started to advertise on the radio. His commercials were an immediate success. He wrote his own jingles and they were sung to the tune of "On, Wisconsin."

The customers flocked to his car lot, which by now had grown to more than ten acres of plastic and neon signs, as well as several hundred shiny used cars. Lindley had six full-time salesmen working for him, and he required that they all wear cowboy hats just like his.

As Lindley's business fortunes improved, his standing in the community went up as well. He joined the Elks, the country club, and the American Legion. He became a deacon at the Doublewide Church of Highway 54. There was only one mountain left for him to climb; his sole remaining ambition was to star in his very own television commercial and have it run on Ted Turner's Superstation. He would fantasize about people in Utah and Lipham, West Virginia, hearing his commercial. He not only wanted to be rich; he wanted to be famous.

When his first TV commercial finally ran, the response was more than he had ever dared hope for. Not only was his lot filled with customers, but he had telephone calls from all over the country. He even had a call from Ernest Angley praising him for his religious approach to selling cars, and asking him for a donation to help feed starving children in Vermont. Lindley told the evangelist that his cash flow was a little tight, but that he would make him a great deal on a used Jeepster. Mr. Angley declined to buy the Jeepster, but promised to send Lindley an all-weather bookmark to use in his Bible.

One day, Lindley got a call from Detroit. The caller told Lindley who he was and indicated that he had a great business deal for him. He wanted Lindley to meet him at the Atlanta airport to discuss the possibility of making him rich beyond his wildest dreams. Lindley, doing his best "Price is Right" imitation, screamed into the phone, "Come on down." When Lindley hung up the phone, he was actually trembling with anticipation. "Just think . . . a huge auto company wants me to open a dealership. What else could it be?"

The days until the meeting dragged by, and on the appointed day, our hero was right there waiting for the automobile executive to get off the plane.

They went to a nearby restaurant for lunch. They had a drink, then lunch, then another drink. The executive finally lit a cigar, leaned back in his chair and after blowing smoke toward the ceiling, said, "Mr. Aaron, how would you like . . . "

At that point, Lindley interrupted and said, "Call me Uncle Lindley."

The executive went on, "Mr. Aaron, how would you like to own your very own new car dealership?"

Lindley said, "Hot damn! A dream come true! My very own dealership. I can't believe it! Thank you, Jesus, thank you God! Thank you Ted Turner!"

The executive managed to calm Lindley enough to continue. He said, "Mr. Aaron, my company is willing to let you in on a ground-floor opportunity. We're introducing a new car, not a new model you understand, but a new make of automobile. It's the first new make we have introduced in many years, and Mr. Aaron, if you can raise enough money to buy a dealership, the Ford motor company would like you to be the nation's first Edsel dealer."

"Can I do it?" shouted Lindley, "You bet your yankee ass I can do it. I'll borrow on everything I own. I can just see it now . . . Uncle Lindley's Edsel . . . I'll make millions . . . maybe billions!" Lindley was standing now, shouting and waving his arms. "I'll be the most famous car deal-

er in America . . . NO! NO! in the world! I can
see it now . . . me, Lindley M. Aaron, a guest
on the Carson show . . . I know, I know . . . I'll
sponsor the Nightly News. I can see it now . . .
the news is brought to you by Uncle Lindley's
Edsel . . . America's first and best Edsel dealer. Know what I'm going to do? I'll tell you
what I'm going to do. I'm going to fire that lib-
eral ass Dan Rather. I simply won't have him
giving my news . . . "

The car executive said, "Mr. Aaron, the first
thing you've got to do is raise the money. Then
and only then can you become rich and famous."

When lunch was over, Lindley put the executive on an airplane and headed straight for the
bank. He borrowed money on everything he
owned . . . business, home, life insurance,
everything! Uncle Lindley went into hock right
up to the brim of his cowboy hat.

Today, there are no longer any Edsel deal-
erships and Dan Rather is still employed.
Lindley is still employed, too, and if you'd like
to meet him, just call the Little Giant Vacuum
Cleaner Company. Chances are, he'll be right
out to your house.

There's a lesson here most Southerners have
taken to heart. You can serve God, or you can
serve Mammon. But if you try to use God to serve
Mammon, you're liable to end up as cannon fod-
der for Dan Rather.

★ SOUTHERN FUNERALS ★

The Deep South is really into funerals. We do a lot of things at funerals that are warm, loving, and wonderful. We also do some things that are just too tacky to be believed. On the wonderful side: all the neighbors show up to hug and give comfort as best they can. When they show up, they always—and I mean always—bring food. They know that people will be coming from miles around, and there must be a feast waiting when they arrive. They offer to "put up" any out-of-town guest that the bereaved doesn't have room for, and all in all, it's great when close friends surround the grieving family with as much love and comfort as they are able to give.

Let's now get to the tacky: I have never quite understood it, but it is not uncommon at all to take photographs of the deceased in his coffin. When video cameras became readily available, they quickly started to show up at Southern funerals. It is common practice to see old Uncle Clarence with his video camera, not only getting a close up of the recently departed, but of all the mourners in the church and at graveside squalling their eyes out. I don't know at what occasion these movies are replayed; I can only assume that if you wish to make someone completely miserable, you drag out your collection of funeral film. It seems to me that it would be more fun to go into town and watch the water tank leak.

Some widows think it is their responsibility to add spice to the festivities. In the midst of one North Carolina funeral, while the minister was preaching, the new widow made a dash from the front pew to the open coffin and crawled up on the corpse, wailing and screaming, "Oh, I can't live without you . . . don't leave me" (there was every indication that he had already left). She was helped back to her seat, only to bolt forward again and try to pull her late husband from the coffin. This bizarre ritual was repeated three times; each time she screamed louder and evoked more pity from the assembly. The kicker to this story is that she was remarried exactly three days after the funeral.

A brand new preacher in Alpharetta, Georgia, opened the service by saying, "Dearly beloved, people are dying now who have never died before."

I don't guess there is any other part of the country where people take their sports as seriously as they do in the South, and this obsession seems to carry over into Southern funerals. I heard recently of a man being buried wearing an Atlanta Braves baseball hat.

Football fans are often buried in coffins that are designed with their college colors—both inside and outside—and for just a few dollars more, a school crest can be had on the inside lid of the coffin.

In Alabama, one particularly rabid fan was buried with a picture of the famed Alabama coach Bear Bryant clutched in his hands.

I guess the tackiest thing I ever heard of was a funeral in Ashville, North Carolina. Someone took a portable radio to the church for the memorial service, and during the entire eulogy an automobile race roared in the background.

Prior to the final closing of the casket, one Southern widow stood before the coffin for about ninety seconds saying her final goodbye. She told the corpse that she had loved him more than anybody had ever been loved before. She went on and on about their wonderful life together and closed her farewell by saying, " . . . and Fred, I can honestly say that I wouldn't have you back for a million tax-free dollars."

One funeral service in Georgia was interrupted

when a non-family mourner stood up in the middle of the church and announced to a startled minister, "I must sing taps." Before the minister could regain his composure, she started in on an incredibly off-key rendition of the old military standard. Like good, polite Southern people, everybody sat very quietly while she made a complete fool of herself.

A grieving widow in Glynn County, Georgia, bought a very expensive suit for her beloved husband to be buried in. According to all who knew, it was said to be, by far, the most expensive suit the deceased had ever had on. For some reason known only to her, the widow decided that the funeral director had switched to a cheaper suit before her husband was laid to rest. She worried and stewed about it for several days and then actually had her husband's body exhumed to determine if the expensive suit had been switched. It had not.

A Gwinnett County, Georgia, funeral was held up when two of the pallbearers got into a fist fight between the hearse and the gravesite. They simply sat the coffin down in the street and got into a bloody fight. Unfortunately, nobody had thought to bring a video camera.

Nothing could be as tacky as a New Orleans jazz funeral. I know it's tradition, but by my yardstick, it is a very tacky tradition. I passed a funeral procession there once that was en route from the church to the cemetery. The third car back from the hearse was a Ford convertible with the top down.

In one Southern family, there were three aunts who were all known for fainting at funerals. Their swoons were so predictable that at every funeral, each aunt had someone assigned to be with her for the duration. The helpers' duty was to catch the aunts when they fainted. These three young men became known as "catchers" and became a fixture at every family funeral.

The new rage at rural Southern funerals is a wreath with a plastic telephone in the middle. In large letters on a ribbon is the message, "Jesus called and Mama answered."

And how can anyone ever forget the funeral with a cassette recorder blaring, "I did it my way"?

I will close this chapter with what I believe to be the last word in tackiness. When his wife passed away, the surviving husband granted her last wish and had her cremated. This is perfectly acceptable. Now comes the bizarre part . . . When the widower realized that proper Southern manners required that he send thank-you notes to everyone who had sent flowers, he didn't want to send plain old thank-you notes, so he bought a bunch of little bitty baggies. He put a pinch of his late wife's ashes, along with one petal from the flowers he had received, into each little baggie and mailed them in lieu of thank-you notes.

North or South, I don't see how anybody is ever going to top that.

★ WHAT IS YOUR ★ DENOMINATION?

I have talked and written much about eating. I have given recipes, recommended good restaurants, and told the secrets of good eating from coast to coast.

I don't like to appear immodest, but when it comes to eating, I consider myself an expert.

I learned what good food is supposed to be at an early age, mostly by attending what we call in the South "dinner on the grounds."

I not only attended those functions at my church, but at almost every denomination in Christendom. If anyone ever invited me to be a visitor on a Sunday that included dinner on the grounds, I was there. On any one of these Sundays, you can find the most wonderful food anywhere. The ladies of the church take this occasion to pull out all the stops and bring their specialty dish.

It is not uncommon at all to see a table forty or fifty feet long with food covering every square inch. The very sight of this table is enough to make a visiting glutton feel like a stranger in paradise. There is so much food that it usually cannot be eaten in one meal. It should properly be called "dinner and supper on the grounds."

Preachin' usually starts about 11 a.m. and lasts until roughly noon. Everyone then goes outside and after a long, long blessing, dinner is served.

About 1:30 or 1:45 p.m. the leftovers are covered with snow-white tablecloths, and the grown-ups wander little by little back into the church for some good old-fashioned singing. The children usually stay outside and run and play as the afternoon wears on. Folks come and go from the singing to the table. I'm not sure how many people have ever been brought to the foot of the Cross by attending an all-day singing and dinner on the grounds, but I've never seen anyone leave who was not full and smiling.

You may not believe this, but due to the many happy hours that I have spent involved in one or another church's dinner on the grounds, I am able to tell you a cook's religious persuasion just by tasting his or her cooking. This ability isn't come by easily. You must spend many hours in research and study. You must taste each dish carefully and make mental notes. After exhaustive research, you learn that there are some gastronomic truisms—for example:

- String beans: Methodists are far and away the best string bean cooks. They know that the only artful way to fix string beans is to cook them almost to death. When the beans are starting to turn black, then and only then are they served. My Methodist friends all seem to smile a lot. I give their string beans a good part of the credit.

- Fried chicken: This is no contest. I have never had any fried chicken that I didn't like, but if you want world-class fried chicken, you need to find some that was cooked by a Baptist. They know that, basically, "grease is our friend." They know that eating chicken with a thick crust can give you a closer walk with your Maker. Any Baptist preacher will tell you that the two things you need to get through life are a Bible and fried chicken, and to know what to do with both of them.

- Hams and roasts: My Episcopalian friends are best with hams and roasts. Especially when it comes to top-dollar cuts, Episcopalians wrote the book on these fine meats.

- Spicy food: It goes without saying that the most delicious spicy foods are likely to have been prepared by a Catholic.

A few more facts that you might find useful in your research:

- Church of Christ members tend to serve cornbread while Presbyterians almost always serve rolls.

- The smaller the church, the better the potato salad.

- The larger the church, the better the creamed corn.

- Cakes, pies and banana pudding are the desserts of choice among most denominations.

I don't guess telling someone's religious preference by their cooking will ever become an

Olympic event, but the research sure is fun. Besides, it's a great way to get religion, and some people need more religion than others.

★ A SOUTHERN ★ MISCELLANY

★ KUDZU ★

I don't know how many acres of land in the South have been taken over by kudzu, but it must be in the millions. It covers the shoulders of the road, old farm houses, abandoned cars, and just about everything else.

There seems to be no way to kill it. It is tougher than a ten-cent steak, and no matter how you fight it, kudzu always seems to come out the winner.

The following is the true account of how kudzu came to our beloved Southland, as well as the shocking answer to one of this nation's most baffling mysteries.

Kudzu was originally brought here by a Japanese gentleman named Hershell Lamar Kudzu, a seed salesman from Tokyo. Old Hershell convinced some farmers that they could plant kudzu and use it as cattle feed. It was a new idea and not an easy sale, but he explained to them that kudzu could grow faster than the cattle could eat it. What he didn't tell them, however, was that kudzu could also grow faster than a grown man could run. His pitch was successful, and kudzu was planted all over the South.

Now, one of the great unsolved mysteries concerns Amelia Earhart's disappearance. Old-timers, however, know the truth. Just before she was supposed to take off on her around-the-world trip, she walked out into the edge of a kudzu field to take a whiz. It was a horrible thing to watch. The kudzu got her, it got her airplane, it also got a midget who was playing "Lady of Spain" on a little bitty accordion.

You see, what Hershell Lamar didn't tell anybody was that cows don't eat kudzu, but kudzu will flat eat a cow.

★ POSSUMS ★

Most Southerners that I know seem to feel a certain kinship with possums. I'm really not sure why, 'cause they're not good for much of anything. They're not fit to eat no matter how you fix 'em. They would never make a good pet; they're surly, slow, awkward and ugly. I think we feel that kinship because we feel sorry for them.

It may sound strange that anybody could feel sorry for a possum, but I have felt for a long time that possums as a species are suicidal. If you don't believe it, just check the highways. You will find that thousands of possums spend their spare time jumping in front of cars. I've given the subject a great deal of thought. I think I have figured out why they take their own lives, and I don't blame them. They have nothing to live for because they have nothing to look forward to. They cannot look forward to breeding because the only thing they have to breed with is another possum. Think about that for a minute. They can't look forward to becoming Mother or Daddy possums 'cause all their babies are going to be possums, and the only thing uglier than a grown possum is a baby possum.

Do you think life would be worthwhile if all your friends and associates were possums? Can you imagine going to a Rotary Club meeting and finding the guest speaker is a possum?

Yes sir, possums are definitely suicidal, and I don't blame 'em.

★ FORD VERSUS ★ CHEVROLET

In the South of my youth, there were only two kinds of men: those who drove Fords and those who drove Chevrolets. And the debate over the relative merits of these two brands never ceased. There were, of course, other makes of vehicle, but no real Southerner would consider owning one. Plymouth was regarded as an off-brand, and the Nash was looked down upon because they also made refrigerators (Kelvinator). Driving a Studebaker was like wetting the bed—you weren't blamed for it, but at the same time you were expected to feel ashamed.

In the old days, most small Southern towns had a Ford dealership and a Chevrolet dealership. The product loyalty of the customers was not to be believed, and many an argument got underway something like this:

"Is that a Chevrolet you're drivin'? I had a Chevrolet once . . . weakest car I ever owned. Wouldn't pull a sick whore off a slop jar."

"Oh yeah? I'd rather have a sister in a cathouse than a brother driving a Ford."

It was at this point that a bystander with a cooler head would chime in and say, "Come on, you guys . . . you're fussin' over something silly."

"Silly? Silly? What do you know, you dumb ass? You drive a DeSoto. That ain't even a real car. I'd rather have a social disease than be in the same used car lot with a DeSoto."

Right about now the local Southern sage would take a draw on his pipe, blow smoke in the air and say, "I'd rather walk barefoot through a chicken house carrying a Chevrolet hubcap than own the best Ford ever made."

I never heard anyone top that.

THE POTBELLIED
★ STOVE ★

The old potbellied stove was a fixture in my
South until recent years.

Before the days of more convenient heating,
the potbellied stove held court in almost all public places. It was made of cast iron and burned
either wood or coal. Every small Southern
town depot, courthouse, and general store
had one, and in the wintertime it became the
gathering place for every old-timer in town. It
was around this old stove that most of the
world's problems were solved. Like most of
the wonderful things of my childhood, it fell vic-
tim to progress. Did you ever see anybody
solve a problem sitting around an automatic
heater? What price progress?

★ THE FRONT PORCH ★

I don't guess that the front porch was invented in the South, but I am convinced that we held it in more reverence than any other part of the country. We took pride in the way our porches looked. We painted them every couple of years and washed them with soapy water every couple of weeks. We gathered there on warm summer evenings to listen to the radio. We planted wisteria vines to give shade, and we furnished them with rocking chairs and a glider.

The front porch was a great place to sit, read the Sunday paper, and wave at cars going by. Your girlfriend's porch was a wonderful place to sit and hope that her mother would turn out the porch light so that you could conduct a brief test of the girl's will power.

Lemonade even tasted better on that old front porch.

It's very hard for me to think about growing

up in a world without front porches. In the New South, porches have been replaced for the most part by patios and decks. It's difficult to take pride in a patio or a deck. That's why people put them in the back of the house where nobody can see them.

I have high hopes that Southern builders will return to their senses and start building front porches on houses again. The fireplace and the ceiling fan have made a comeback. That gives me hope for the return of the porch.

★ THE GENERAL STORE ★

I know it's my failing memory, but it seems to me that in the South of my childhood, things were better. The stores are a good example of this. Whenever I go into one of our modern convenience stores, I like the fact that everything is clean and that you can get right in and out in about two minutes. They stock about everything you need from toothpicks to a cold six-pack. The only problem I find with them is that they lack the character and personality of the old general store.

The general store had the same person behind the counter day in and day out, year in and year out. Not so with the convenience store. If you were a regular customer at a general store, the proprietors knew you by name and knew that they depended on you for their livelihood. They knew you so well that you could open a charge account without even asking. Every time you bought something, the person behind the counter would say, "Cash or charge?" If you said, "Charge," bingo!—you had just opened an account. It was just that simple. No forms were filled out or questions asked; they were unnecessary. The folks there knew you would be back on payday to settle up. It was a nice way to do business.

General stores were everywhere, and while they were all a little different, they were fundamentally alike. They were so much alike, in fact, that you might think the same person owned them all.

The general store was always wood frame. A brick general store would have been completely out of place. There were always two gas pumps out front. One said "Ethyl" and one said "Regular." There was also a kerosene dispenser where you could buy a dime's worth of kerosene. The store had double screen doors with writing on them that, more often than not, said, "Colonial is Good Bread." Tied to the top of the screen door was a fist-sized wad of cotton. It was thought that this would keep the flies and bugs out.

Once inside the store, you saw a lot of other signs—signs that said things like "Tube Rose Snuff," "I'd walk a mile for a Camel," or "RC Cola, Best by Taste Test." They tried their best to stock whatever you could ever want or need, from hoop cheese to cow feed and everything in between. They even had a punchboard where, for a dime, you could try your luck at winning a single-shot .22 rifle. Second prize was a picture of President Roosevelt suitable for framing. There was a sign on the counter that told you to buy two cans of Prince Albert smoking tobacco and get a genuine briar pipe absolutely free.

The store was not real clean, however, because of the potbellied stove, and there was fly paper hanging from the ceiling. The canned goods were dusty and the man behind the counter usually needed a shave. I'm sure the health inspector would have had a fit if he had seen their meat department.

In spite of these drawbacks, it was a great place to shop and a part of the South that unfortunately is gone forever.

AMERICA'S FIRST
★ MARATHON ★

Whenever I see the television reports on the
Boston marathon, I am reminded that the
long distance run that we now call a marathon
was first attempted in the Deep South.

Like all things of great import, it happened
by accident. Many years ago in Madison,
Georgia, two teenage brothers decided it would
be great fun to hop a passing freight train. The
train was moving at a pretty good clip, so it was
necessary that the brothers sprint to get on board.

The older brother got to the open box car door
and pulled himself inside only to find that the
car had no floor. He ended up having to run all
the way from Madison to Greensboro, Georgia,
and in the process became the world's first long
distance runner.

★ THE GOURD DIPPER ★

The gourd dipper is still in widespread use in the South. Like everyone else who ever had a drink of well water out of a gourd dipper, I know that it is special. I have never understood why anyone would drink water out of anything else. Why are the kitchen cabinets of America full of glasses when one gourd dipper per family could put all of us in the water drinking business *and* make us the envy of the crown heads of Europe?

★ THE MYTH OF ★ CHITTERLINGS

There is a myth in the north concerning hog innards. I mean, of course, chitterlings (pronounced chitlins). The myth would have folks believe that chitterlings are eaten by everyone in the South, every day. The fact of the matter is that you seldom see or hear much about them. The reason is that they are not fit to eat. There is no way to cook them so as to make them taste good.

People have been trying to get me to eat them for years. I would rather eat a Motorola radio.

★ SOUTHERN WISDOM ★

- The trouble with being poor is that it takes up all your time.

- This country started going to Hell when they moved the dimmer button off the floorboard.

- Never make fun of a Southerner nick-named "Frog." He got that name because he likes to croak people.

- Being Southern is not a state of mind. It's where you were, by God, born.

- In the South, you are never a man until your daddy tells you you are a man.

- Southerners almost never use the word *whom.* They know that if you use it properly, you sound pretentious. If you use it improperly, you sound stupid.

- It is better to have died as a small child than to serve your guest unsweetened iced tea.

- Blessed are those who hug.

- A good education is important. It's the only way you can be sure of getting a job in the shade.

- Smile more, because sunshine is good for your teeth.

- If there is more than one way to skin a cat, I don't want to know about it.

- True Southern cooking will stick to your ribs . . . or anything else it touches.

- Contrary to popular opinion, certain parts of Florida are in the South after all.

POSTSCRIPT:
★ THE OLD REBEL ★

I can't remember the first time I heard someone say, "You people are still fighting the Civil
War." Nothing could be further from the truth.
It would take a complete fool for any Southerner
to want to fight that war again. They licked us
good and proper, and we know and completely understand that.

To illustrate this point, I offer the following
song written by a Confederate veteran named
Innes Randolph. It's called "The Old Rebel," and
its tune goes something like "A Ramblin' Wreck
from Georgia Tech."

> Oh, I'm a good old rebel,
> Now that's just what I am;
> For the "fair land of freedom"
> I do not care a damn;
> I'm glad I fit against it,
> I only wish we'd won,
> And I don't want no pardon
> For anything I done.
>
> I hate the Constitution,
> This great Republic, too;
> I hate the freedman's buro

In uniforms of blue;
I hate the nasty eagle
With all his brags and fuss;
The lyin' thievin' yankees,
I hate 'em wuss and wuss.

I hate the yankee nation
And everything they do;
I hate the Declaration
Of Independence, too.
I hate the glorious Union,
'Tis dripping with our blood;
I hate the striped banner—
I fit it all I could.

I followed old Marse Robert
For four years nearabout;
Got wounded in three places,
And starved on Point Lookout.
I cotch the roomatism
A-campin' in the snow,
But if I killed a chance of yankees,
I'd like to kill some mo'.

Three hundred thousand yankees
Is stiff in Southern dust;
We got three hundred thousand
Before they conquered us;
They died of Southern fever
And Southern steel and shot;

I wish it was three million,
Instead of what we got.

I can't take up my musket
And fight 'em now no more,
But I ain't a-goin' to love 'em,
Now that is certain sure.
And I don't want no pardon
For what I was and am;
I won't be reconstructed,
And I don't give a damn.

So . . . the next time you accuse someone of still fighting the Civil War, remember the composer of this song. Even he was no longer fighting the war . . . although he damn sure would have liked to have been.